The Pleasure of God's Company

A HANDBOOK FOR LEADING INTERCESSIONS AT THE EUCHARIST

Paul Iles

Kevin Mayhew

First published in Great Britain by
KEVIN MAYHEW LTD
Rattlesden
Bury St Edmunds
Suffolk
IP30 0SZ

ISBN 0 86209 145 4

Front Cover: *The Holy Trinity* by Andrei Rublev
(c. 1370-1430). Reproduced by kind permission of
Tretjakoff-Galerie, Moscow/Bridgeman Art Library,
London.

Cover design by Graham Johnstone
Printed and bound in Great Britain.

CONTENTS

Introduction 9
Part One
Creative Desire: what is intercession? 14
First things first: some historical background 22
Belief and Prayer: our understanding of God
and our praying 30
Pray without ceasing: difficulties and
misunderstandings which easily hinder 40

Part Two
Called to lead 52
Map-work 61
Practical hints and tips 70
Forms of Intercession 78
Litanies 82
Further resources 89
Musical settings of Responses to Intercessions 90
Book List 95

Acknowledgements

The publishers wish to express their gratitude to the following for permission to reproduce extracts from the following publications:

Collins Liturgical Publications, 8 Grafton Street, London W1X 3LA for extracts from *Praying Together in Word and Song* © Les Presses de Taize (France)

Darton, Longman and Todd, 89 Lillie Road, London SW6 1UD for extracts from *Becoming What I am* by H.A. Williams, CR; and *School for Prayer* by Anthony Bloom

Hamish Hamilton Ltd, 27 Wrights Lane, London W8 5TZ for extracts from *End of a Journey* by Philip Toynbee

A R Mowbray and Co Ltd, Artillery Row, London SW1P 1RT for extracts from *Intercessions for use with Series 1 & 2 or 3 Holy Communion* by Colin Semper

Oxford University Press, Walton Street, Oxford OX2 6DP for extracts from *The Epistle to the Romans* by Karl Barth, translated by E.C. Hoskyns; and *Michael Ramsey, A Life* by Owen Chadwick

The Society for the Promotion of Christian Knowledge, Marylebone Road, London NW1 4DU for extracts from *Confessions of a Conservative Liberal* by John Habgood

AUTHOR'S NOTE

I am grateful to all those who have helped me with this book, and particularly I wish to thank Judy Whitehead who has provided the line drawings to accompany the first four chapters. Prayer is triggered, articulated and sustained in many different ways. I believe her drawings will release feelings and imagination which cannot be reached through words.

I have myself made the suggestions about the music, but I am very conscious that the choice reflects my own taste which is likely to be restricted and not shared by everyone. I wish I could be more cosmopolitan and add suggestions from a much wider spectrum of musical styles. However, I do urge you to disregard my choices if they do not speak to you. Every style of music has some potential for opening up the feelings and imagination which nourish our vision of God. I hope you will take the theme word and first explore the music you enjoy, looking for whatever speaks to you of the theme. Then it may well be worth your while to listen to my choices and discover if they too can carry you further.

FOREWORD

'The Church gathers for worship and scatters for mission.' The rhythm of our Christian life is to assemble before God to offer the sacrifice of praise and thanksgiving and to disperse into the world to witness to Him and serve Him. We gather in obedience to the command: 'Do this in remembrance of me.' We scatter in order to 'go into all the world and preach the gospel to the whole creation.'

In the offering of worship we are conscious of our personal needs: our longing to praise and adore God, to receive His forgiveness, to attend to His word and be renewed and transformed in the likeness of Christ through receiving the sacrament. Yet our worship is not individualistic but corporate. We are persons in community. Worship is the Church's offering, and the needs of the Church's ministry and its engagement in mission, both locally and globally, feature largely in our prayers. And it is right that this should be so. But the world not the church is God's first love. As worshippers we bring into His presence the cares and concerns of the world which He creates and redeems; the world we belong to, and in which we live and work. Our prayer is offered on the world's behalf. This book is concerned with the prayer of intercession. Canon Iles following Archbishop Ramsey reminds us that intercession means 'to be with someone on behalf of others.' The risen and ascended Christ, in and with whom we pray, 'is with the Father with the world on his heart, with all of us on his heart.'

Many books have been written on the use and exposition of scripture in worship, and still more on the nature of Eucharistic worship. Comparatively few have centered on the prayers on intercession.

Canon Iles is to be thanked and congratulated on meeting a real need. He provides a helpful introduction to the rationale of intercessory prayer, not forgetting the cost and demands that such prayer imposes on those who offer it. And drawing from his wide pastoral experience in parishes, schools and cathedrals he puts before us invaluable suggestions on the preparation and presentation of intercession in Sunday worship: the range of content, different styles, the choice of words, the use of silence, and he gives a large number of practical hints. I believe that many parish clergy, readers, and worship leaders will find this little book a useful aid in teaching about prayer and in the ordering of a most important element in our public worship. I pray that its lessons may be heeded and the content of our worship consequently deepened and enriched.

+ **Colin Winton:**

FOR A.G.
called to pray
and to help others to pray

Introduction

The worshipping Christian community, or the People of God, is now understood to be the whole group of those baptised, men and women, called and commissioned as ministers of the Gospel to witness to God and, in his name, to serve the world.

With this deepening understanding of the Ministry of the whole Christian community, every disciple is now finding himself or herself in church, Sunday by Sunday, tackling tasks which many have never attempted before and which require skills for which there is little, if any, formal training.

This book offers guidance about how to undertake what may be, in some ways, the hardest — to lead The Prayers of the Faithful (as intercession is traditionally and historically known) at the Eucharist.

The Gospel is full of promise, 'When the time comes, the words you need will be given you; for it is not you who will be speaking; it will be the Spirit of your Father speaking in you' (Matthew 10, 19b-20). Although here Jesus was telling the disciples of the inspiration Christians can rely on when they have to testify to their faith under persecution, it's not misreading the text to say that the same promise can also strengthen those called to lead prayer in public worship. St Paul's comment about Life in the Spirit also brings confidence: 'the Spirit comes to the aid of our weakness. We do not even know how we ought to pray, but through our inarticulate groans the Spirit himself is pleading for us' (Romans 8: 26).

All effective Christian ministry depends above all on the combined sense of being *both called and equipped* by God to discharge it. And it can be done in confidence and trust when we turn to the Spirit and rely on him for the necessary gifts, entirely at his disposal, which he readily distributes.

There is, though, a right and proper place for self-help. Reading scripture in public, helping with the distribution of the holy communion, being called on to lead the prayers of intercession are all tasks not to be undertaken lightly and without proper preparation.

The advice given here is intended to be as practical as possible and therefore some will find it too obvious and tedious. However, I hope many will agree that what is obvious to some often remains a mystery to others, until it is spelt out in some shape or form. A D.I.Y. guide is bound to be about basics.

But this practical approach should not obscure the need for three often 'hidden virtues' which are equally essential. Firstly, those who lead inter-cessions will depend on and seek personal growth in their own prayer-life and developing spirituality and sensitivity. Secondly, they will need to be able to be part of a team of leaders who conduct public worship (ordained and lay) and therefore need the ability to fit in with others and work alongside them. And thirdly, they will need to develop the particular quality of leadership within the Christian commun-ity which is representative rather than individual.

Thus this booklet is divided into two parts — theory and practice, if you like.

Part 1 attempts to open up the background of intercessory prayer — its purpose, its history, and its theological basis. The four sections can be used separately, either by individual leaders of intercession for their own personal preparation, or as outlines for group study and discussion leading into prayer. At the end of each section in part 1,

I offer three things to help carry the study forward: passages for further thought, from scripture and other sources, suggestions about music which might be helpful as a non-verbal source of imagination, openness and growth, and a drawing which is intended to do through the eye the same as the music does through the ear.

Part 2 offers suggestions about the way to stand up and do it — how to prepare and work out the intercessions for the week by quiet thought, gathering together material for the prayer, how to sketch out and choose the words, selecting some and discarding others, how to draw silence, and sometimes music, into the prayer.

There is no reason why the two parts should be read in that order. Some may prefer to go straight to part 2, the practical advice, and turn back to the more reflective section later.

I have restricted myself strictly to conducting the intercessions at a parish eucharist with all the constraints of time and place, which usually means the service will last not much more than an hour and the intercession about five minutes.

Although unlikely in normal circumstances on a Sunday morning, some periods of intercessory prayer on certain occasions may be long enough for the prayer to merge into meditation, and there is a good deal of material available now to help this development; some of it may be found in the report *Patterns for Worship* produced recently by the Church of England Liturgical Commission.[1] Some suggestions for intercession include the use of special lighting effects, movement and dance, slides and other visual and aural aids. I would encourage such experiments wherever possible (although they must never become patronising or fussy), but for the time being I have assumed they cannot be part of the regular task of leading intercession at the Eucharist Sunday by Sunday.

[1]At the time of writing, April 1990, *Patterns for Worship* is available only as a report in response to the House of Bishops, and none of its contents is yet authorised or commended for liturgical use.

Part One

——— **Creative Desire** ———

The Great Intercession is a prayer of creative desire;
desire that the whole world may be
brought to the altar of God and made ardent by
the flame of His Charity, transforming all the
activities and institutions of men, and making them
a part of the Kingdom of Heaven.

Evelyn Underhill

I

I once heard Christian Prayer defined quite simply
as time spent in the remembered presence of
God. If so, then prayer contains words and silence,
action and stillness, public and private aspiration.
Beyond these particular aspects of prayer, and
holding it all in place, there is the simple fact of
being together, in company, with God and with
others who also enjoy being with him, which clearly
comes close to the heart of the matter.

This book is about one aspect of the pleasure
of being with God — intercession. When we enjoy
being with God and become more aware of his
presence and love, naturally, he addresses us and
invites us to speak with him. Two people in
relationship can often dispense with chatter and be
silent together happily for quite a long time, and
yet they will need 'the gentle art of conversation'
too. 'Let your requests be made known unto God',
urges St Paul.

Over and over again we are taught that God
knows us better than we know ourselves, and yet,

in spite of this total and intimate knowledge of all he has made, God enjoys conversation with us and delights in it.

For the pleasure of keeping company with God is mutual. There is a sense in which he needs it, too. 'One is one and all alone and evermore shall be so'. But God is not like that: alone and aloof. God is trinity and needs what that implies of interchange and mutuality.

So God engages in dialogue with us, and encourages us to name names in our prayers and to be bold and demanding in saying, as loud as we can, what it is we want.

Jesus himself first insisted we should 'Ask'. He encourages us to think of God not only as Father, but also as the one who gives, who opens, who enables us to find what we are looking for and need. Basic to the character of the God to whom we pray is that he gives, gladly, generously, usually 'more than either we desire or deserve', 'good measure, pressed down and overflowing'. This willing, unrestrained giving is an expression of his unending love and care for his creation.

To admit that desire is one of the roots of prayer may be disturbing at first. Most of us find desire of any kind difficult to handle. In the context of prayer it seems to put the emphasis too much on self rather than on God: something we are taught not to do.

But human beings are always creatures of desire and it is God who has made us this way. True,

15

we can corrupt desire and reduce it to appetite. Often our desires will need to be purified, deepened and transformed. But precisely because desires are God-given, we need not fear their pull: provided, of course, we do all we can to make sure they are harmonised with what God desires for us.

Creative desire, then, is one of the roots of intercessory prayer: that dialogue or conversation with God in which all are invited to take part.

II

In a very familiar communion hymn, we sing of, and to, Jesus —
Intercessor, friend of sinners,
Earth's Redeemer, plead for me,
pointing us to another root of intercession, which is the prayer of Jesus himself.

He prayed for others throughout his ministry on earth, and even while he suffered and died on the Cross, and his praying for mankind continues now he is the Risen Christ. 'Sitting at the right hand of God' may be an image difficult to transpose into contemporary idiom, but whatever else it means, it is not a state of idleness. Jesus remains present with God in the power of continuing activity.
'He is able for all time to save those who
draw near to God through him, since he
always lives to make intercession for them'.
(Hebrews 7:25)

Just as we learn to forgive others, at least partly by grasping first that we ourselves have been forgiven, we interceed for others knowing that Christ is already and always interceeding for us all. Any prayers of intercession we pray are part of his prayer and the prayers of the great company on earth and in heaven of those who pray with him. Sometimes loneliness accompanies prayer but never isolation.

Effective intercession is powerful also because of Jesus' resurrection; it is part of the victory of Easter; one of the fruits of Jesus' victory over evil and one of the gifts which he shares with his friends:
Hitherto you have asked nothing in my name; ask, and you will receive, that your joy may be full (John 16, 24).

III

Any desire we have for God is not enough in itself. The longing for God must be accompanied by a willingness to accept the cost of discipleship. Bringing together desire and discipleship opens the way for God to answer our prayer and fill us with all the richness of being which he wants us to enjoy. Our part in the work of intercession will be as costly to ourselves as it was to Jesus. Faithfully to interceed for others is part of taking up our cross — *daily*, as St Luke reminds us to do.

St Augustine sets the same, clear compass-bearing for all intercessory prayer:
God does not ask us to tell him our needs that he may learn about them, but in order that we may be capable of receiving what he is preparing to give.

For further reading and thought

A Theme Word — Desire

I love the Lord because he heard my voice:
the voice of my supplication;
because he inclined his ear to me:
on the day that I called to him.
                              (Psalm 116: 1-2)

The Spirit maketh intercession for us with
groanings which cannot be uttered.
We wait: but, because we wait upon God,
    our waiting is not in vain.
We look out: but, because we have first
    been observed, we do not look out into
    the void.
We speak: but, because there emerges in our
    speech that which cannot be uttered, we
    do not idly prattle.
And so also we pray.
        (Karl Barth, *The Epistle to the Romans)*

God and man ... are actually and for ever
Two, the two partners of the primal
relationship that, from God to man, is called
mission and commandment; from man to
God, seeing and hearing; between both,
knowledge and love. And in this relationship
the son, although the father dwells and
works in him, bows before him that is
'greater' and prays to him. All modern
attempts to reinterpret this primal actuality
of dialogue and to make of it a relationship
of the I to the self or something of that sort,
as if it were a process confined to man's self-

18

sufficient inwardness, are vain and belong to
the abysmal history of deactualisation.

(Martin Buber)

And slowly answered Arthur from the barge:
'The old order changeth, yielding place to
    new,
And God fulfils Himself in many ways,
Lest one good custom should corrupt the
    world.
Comfort thyself: what comfort is in me?
I have lived my life, and that which I have
    done
May He within Himself make pure! but thou,
If thou should'st never see my face again,
Pray for my soul. More things are wrought
    by prayer
Than this world dreams of. Wherefore let thy
    voice
Rise like a fountain for me night and day.
For what are men better than sheep or goats
That nourish a blind life within the brain,
If, knowing God, they lift not hands of
    prayer
Both for themselves and those who call
    them friend?
For so the whole round earth is every way
Bound by gold chains about the feet of
    God'.

(From *Morte D'Arthur*, Alfred Lord Tennyson)

You must want like God that you may be satisfied like God. Were you not made in his image? There is nothing wrong with wanting as such. Our wants, our desires, our loves lead us, if rightly ordered, to God himself. It is a disorder of desire that leads men away from God. When we dote upon the perfections and beauties of some one creature, we do not love that too much, but other things too little. Never was anything in this world loved too much, but many things have been loved in a false way, and all in too short a measure.

(Thomas Traherne)

Music

Bach's *Double Violin Concerto in D minor* provides a marvellous insight through music into the way two people can relate together in complete mutuality with intimacy, trust and joy. The movements also reflect many changing moods within such a relationship.

First Things First

It is meet and right, O Lord, to pray without ceasing and to invoke you who from the beginning have given a gracious and favourable assent to the continual prayer of your servants. To those who call you give before they ask, and prepare for them marvellous works; you do not deny them mercy, but show your goodwill and protection.

Mozarabic Rite

I

The Eucharist is both the principal source of the life of the Church and the principal expression of the worship it offers to God. Within it, intercession has never been optional. Every Christian Liturgy, or eucharist, always contains 'common prayers' for the Church and for the World.

Justin Martyr describing the eucharist as he knew it in Rome, in AD 160, says, 'we send up prayers'. Slightly later, Tertullian writing of the Eucharist in Africa says prayers were made 'for the emperor and all in authority, for the condition of the world, for peace and for the delay of the end of all things'.

From the early records of the Christian Church, we know the first task shared in by a newly baptised member of the community was the corporate prayer of the Church.

After we have thus cleansed him who believes and is united to us, we lead him to those who are called brethren where they

are assembled, in order to say common
prayers earnestly, for ourselves, for him who
has been enlightened and for all others
everywhere.

The 'Prayers of the Faithful' were so highly valued that they were carefully guarded by the community. They were not open to the unbaptised, even those under instruction in the faith. Catechumens heard the bible readings and the sermon, but then they were dismissed, before the corporate prayer began. As a sign of their importance to the Christian community, these prayers were brought to a conclusion with the Kiss of Peace.

So two facts stand out. Some form of general intercession has always been *obligatory* in the eucharist and it has always been a *corporate action* by the congregation.

Although every rite includes it, the prayer of intercession appears in a variety of forms and not always at the same point in the order of service. But even when the custom began to decay in the Middle Ages, no eucharist was ever celebrated without intercession. A vestige of the traditional Prayers of the Faithful was left in the Canon of the Mass itself. Eventually, however, this proved to be too brief and inadequate, and Cranmer in his liturgies of 1549 and 1552 attempted to redress the balance.

II

There are three principal forms of general intercession for liturgical use and each gives us a possible method of making intercession — a series of biddings and collects, as recorded in the solemn prayers of Good Friday; a form of litany with a people's response, such as the shorter form of intercession written by Pope Gelasius; and the Bidding Prayer which is the basis of the Prayer for the Whole State of Christ's Church in the Book of Common Prayer.

Firstly, the Good Friday Prayers *(Orationes Solemnis)*. This was a long, solemn set of prayers of intercession divided into nine sections. Each section took the same form:

   The priest announced a subject for prayer by making a bidding
   The deacon invited the people to kneel and pray
   The people prayed together in silence
   The priest summed up the prayers of the community in a collect
   The people stood for the next bidding

A modern version of these solemn prayers can be found in *Lent, Holy Week and Easter* (pages 212-216).

Secondly, the Litany of Pope Gelasius *(Deprecatio Gelasii)*. In the fifth century, Pope Gelasius devised a shorter and more easily accessible form of intercession, basing it on the Deacon's Litany from the ancient eastern rites. The collects were omitted and the people took part

24

verbally simply by making the response *Kyrie Eleison* to each bidding. Usually this prayer was said at the beginning of the Eucharist, which is the reason why the response of the people, *Kyrie Eleison*, still remains in this place in the modern rites. A version of this form of intercession is included in the rite A order of the Eucharist in the *Alternative Service Book*, section 81, though it is now moved from the beginning of the service and placed in the more customary place at the end of the Ministry of the Word.

Thirdly, the Bidding Prayer. This form of intercession was written in the vernacular and permitted variation of wording, making it a more flexible form of intercessory prayer and better adapted to take account of local and particular circumstances. Forms of Bidding Prayer were used in France and England by at least the 11th century, and along with the sermon or homily it was the only part of the Medieval Latin Mass 'in the language of the people'. Cranmer almost certainly had this form of intercession in mind when he devised his *Prayer for the whole state of Christ's Church*.

Other forms of intercession are now being developed. In public worship, however, one or other of these three traditional forms (or a development from them) is still in regular use. Whenever we share in intercessory prayer, it is necessary to decide which of the three forms is being used and not to confuse them. Before the leader begins he or she must choose which form to use. Is it a form of biddings with collects, a form of litany with a response, or a form of bidding prayer?

Sadly, one of the mistakes made in public worship all too often is that the intercessions are led in such a way that they are a mixture of all three types, which helps neither the leader of prayer nor those praying.

For further reading and thought

A theme word — Together

Those who accepted (Peter's) word were baptised, and some three thousand were added to their number that day.
They met constantly to hear the apostles teach, and to share the common life, to break bread, and to pray. A sense of awe was everywhere, and many marvels and signs were brought about through the apostles.   (Acts 2:41-43)

On Sundays there is an assembly of all (Christians) who live in towns or in the country, and the memoirs of the apostles or the writings of the prophets are read as long as time allows.
Then the reading is brought to an end, and the president delivers an address in which he admonishes and encourages us to imitate in our own lives the beautiful lessons we have heard read.
Then we all stand up together and pray. When we have finished the prayer, bread and wine and water are brought up; the president offers prayers and thanksgivings as best he can, and the people say 'Amen' as an expression of their agreement. Then follows the distribution of the food over which the

26

prayer of thanksgiving has been recited, all
present receive some of it, and the deacons
carry some to those who are absent.

(Justin Martyr,
First Apology in defence of Christians,
chapters 66-67)

When we make application to men in high
positions we do not presume to do so
without reverence and humility; how much
more, then, are we bound to entreat God,
the Lord of all, with all humility and devout
purity of heart. And we must recognise that
we are heard not for our much speaking, but
for our purity of heart and tears of
contrition. Therefore our prayer must be
brief and pure — unless it chance to be
prolonged with the inspiration of God's
grace. When we assemble together, let the
prayer be quite brief; and let us all rise
together, when the Prior gives the signal.

(*Rule of St Benedict*
Chapter 20, Of Reverence in Prayer)

God sees into the hearts of those who pray.
What need then, someone will say, that we
should ask God for what we need? Does he
not know already what we need? Why then
should we pray? God does indeed know
what things we need, and with generosity
provides all we need for the refreshment of
our bodies, and since he is good, he sends
down his rains upon the just and the unjust
alike, and causes his sun to shine upon the
good and the bad (Matthew 5, 45), even
before we ask him. But faith, and the power
of virtue, and the Kingdom of Heaven, these

you will not receive unless you ask for them
in labouring and steadfastness.

(St Basil the Great, *Sermon on Prayer*)

Music

Sibelius, String Quartet 'Voces Intimae' —
listening, we gain a picture of four instruments
playing together with complete equality, each one
complements what the others lack and brings
harmony to the whole.

Belief and Prayer

Intercession is only conducted aright if there is a belief that there is a harmony and a love at the heart of the universe which can be trusted. 'If you abide in me and my words abide in you, ask whatever you will and it shall be done for you' (John 15:7).
Colin Semper

I

When people consider Christian doctrine they naturally ask, is it true? When they consider prayer, they want to know does it work?

In the Christian life, believing and praying always go together and depend on each other. No-one has put this better than a great modern theologian: Karl Barth, in his *Evangelical Theology*, says 'the first and basic act of theological work is prayer'.

The truth of doctrine is complex and touches on questions of philosophy, theology, history, sociology and even psychology. The way in which prayer works is equally complex. Not surprisingly most of us 'never cease from exploration' and spend a lifetime wrestling with a growing understanding of prayer.

An invitation to explore something complex may sound daunting, but in the case of exploring belief and prayer we should not be put off. We have been told 'a journey of a thousand miles starts with one step', and Jesus promises his friends that, if they undertake the journey of discipleship, they will come to know the truth and such knowledge will bring them a freedom they can find in no other way.

It is not cheating or short-circuiting debate to say that because Jesus believed in God we can say with equal and direct confidence that we too believe. As each disciple is enabled by the master to do God's will, each discovers the meaning of belief. 'Whoever has the will to do the will of God shall know whether my teaching comes from him or is merely my own' (John 7:17).

Our praying can be based on the same direct confidence. For another promise Jesus made to his friends was that their prayers would unite them with the Father. He would never have made such a statement as an observation from outside his own personal experience. He said it because he knew its truth for himself, from within, and lived with such trust himself. Again, it is not cheating to say, with total directness, we know the effectiveness of prayer because what worked for Jesus also works for us.

There is at least that much simplicity and complexity in understanding how prayer works.

II

Many misunderstandings, though, can arise when we try to put into words, either for ourselves or for other people, how prayer works. This is especially so when we attempt to describe intercession. Any form of praying inexorably reveals the kind of 'god' in which we believe, and how patchy and obscure is our vision of God.

What are the starting points for understanding how intercessory prayer works?

First, we have already said praying is never a solo activity but always corporate, built into the prayer of Christ and the prayer of the Church. This is particularly true whenever we intercede, either in private or in public. From the earliest days Christian congregations have been given the same directive — 'First of all, then, I urge that petitions, prayers, intercessions, and thanksgivings be offered for all men; for sovereigns and all in high office, that we may lead a tranquil and quiet life in full observance of religion and high standards of morality. Such prayer is right, and approved by God our Saviour, whose will it is that all men should find salvation and come to know the truth' (1 Timothy 2: 1-3).

The Prayers of the Faithful are always held firmly within the context of the whole eucharistic action of the Church. Although here we are giving particular attention to intercession, it will mean most and make most sense when we see it as a definite part of this whole. The Leader of the intercessions must also keep this in mind and communicate it to others through the way he leads the prayer.

Second, praying for others is not static — just sitting or kneeling there, listening, wondering what, if anything, will happen as a result of our prayers. It is dynamic — at the very least as a form of genuine conversation with God and with give-and-take on either side; but it is also dynamic because it is a form of participation in the divine activity itself.

God shares his work of creation and redemption with Jesus, and through him, with his friends and disciples. 'My Father has never yet ceased his work, and I am working too' (John 5: 17). He wants us to pray for others on their behalf and seek his will for them, even if we cannot always know what is their need. He wants us to speak with him freely, wrestling with what can happen and what is not yet happening, because it is an expression of the relationship of love and trust and growing understanding between the Father and his sons and daughters.

Third, we need to clarify the kind of activity of God in which we are sharing through prayer. Intercession is not magic or manipulation by the one who prays, either of God or of other people. Instead, through it we discover the power of the Kingdom which is based on weakness and self-giving. Neville Ward writes, 'when the Christian believer prays for others he is penetrating even further into the realm of self-offering'. Only those who recognise and accept the particular power of powerlessness, which is the basis of God's Kingdom, can begin to understand how intercession works.

And finally, too many people think of prayer as an activity of last resort. But asking God for particular things is not panic or desperation, even when it can properly be called a prayer of crisis with the added dimension of urgency which that inevitably brings. But all the requests we make are based on the regular, continuous activity of growing trust in God, whose purposes we believe are being worked out every day.

The Anglican tradition deliberately blends prayer and belief together, each nourishing the other. The experience of praying opens up and enlarges and defines what we believe and reveals what we can go on to believe. On the other hand, as we reflect on what we believe, the method and purpose of our praying will be questioned (sometimes with sharp criticism) and our prayers are strengthened. Wrestling with belief leads to growth in prayer which in turn brings with it the opportunity for new experiences of the activity of God.

For further reading and thought

A Theme Word — Asking

As I was praying for D, sitting down on the stone between bouts of hard digging this afternoon, I felt for the very first time that this intercessory prayer was somehow meshing; connecting; even working. This was partly, perhaps, because of the new method, in which I use my hands with my breathing and praying. But whether it worked to her direct benefit I can't know or even guess.
  (Philip Toynbee, *End of a Journey*, page 102)

But now I find that prayer for D, or Tom, is better if it takes the old form: Have mercy on us — on *us* — rather than on him or on her. True prayer for another should never be *de haut en bas*, from my comparatively all-right state to your misery: it should involve the one who is praying in his own prayer; perhaps — for saints only? — the whole of humanity, past, present and future, should be involved.
  (Philip Toynbee, *ibid*)

If our prayer for others becomes an excuse not to act on their behalf, not to do what we can for them, then of course we can be certain that our prayer is bogus. Real prayer leads to action. But it also saves us from fantasies of omnipotence, of imagining that we can do for people what we manifestly can't do, and from the anxiety and guilt-feelings such fantasies evoke. And praying for people also makes us sensitive to their deepest needs which are generally not their most obvious ones. By means of our prayer God succours people in the very centre and core of their being, and that is what they need most.

(H. A. Williams CR, *Becoming what I am*)

So he said, he would have destroyed them, had not Moses his chosen stood before him in the gap: to turn away his wrathful indignation lest he should destroy them.

(Psalm 106:23)

Read the account of Abraham and his prayer in Genesis 18:16-23

Read this dialogue between Abraham and the Lord and notice (i) the persistence of Abraham's prayer, (ii) the unique relationship it implies between creature and Creator, where both share a particular kind of equality through prayer which does not rob God of his otherness, and (iii) the basis of the bargaining is Abraham's insight into an aspect of the nature of God — the divine responsibility for judgment which itself demands justice.

35

Now let us take a pause and look at this from a slightly different angle: the disciples praying, and us praying as disciples of Jesus. He taught them to pray by giving them the wonderful teaching about prayer, a little of which we have been thinking about; but he taught them to pray even more by being himself the praying one so near to them. What must it have been like to be trying to pray and yet being very near, day by day, night by night, week by week, to Jesus, whose exposure, whose communion with the Heavenly Father was perfect. And in a mysterious way, after Jesus died and rose and ascended into Heaven, they still thought of him as the praying Son of Man. That conviction lies behind the imagery used a little by St Paul, but supremely by the writer of the letter to the Hebrews, of Jesus as the great High Priest ever living to make intercession for us. That image of Jesus as the ceaseless intercessor has entered deeply into our Theology and liturgy. But let us be a little precise about what this imagery means. The Greek verb which we translate intercede doesn't really mean to make petitions or entreaties, it means to 'be with someone on behalf of others' — and what we call the intercession of Jesus ascended, through the ages, really means that he is with the Father with the world on his heart, with all of us on his heart, not begging the Father to be gracious, because it is from the Father that all graciousness ever flows, but being with the Father as it were a kind of channel through which the Father's power and love flow into the world.

(Michael Ramsey)

36

Music

Beethoven, Piano Concerto No 4 — could illustrate the experience of dialogue between creature and Creator, between Abraham and God, and might indicate some of the meaning of conflict, contrast and resolution.

── Pray Without Ceasing ──

Each time you take a human soul with you into your prayer, you accept from God a piece of spiritual work with all its implications and with all its cost — a cost which may mean for you spiritual exhaustion and darkness, and may even include vicarious suffering, the Cross. In offering yourselves on such levels of prayer for the sake of others, you are offering to take part in the mysterious activities of the spiritual world; to share the saving work of Christ.

Evelyn Underhill

I

If we are to ground our prayers in an accurate and sustaining vision of God, who is the Father of our Lord Jesus Christ, it is vital that all intercession should be defined by and directly associated with the Prayers of the Faithful within the Eucharist. This sacrament is a corporate activity of the whole Church, based on the creative and redemptive activity of God and our human response of thanksgiving and service. From it flows all Christian prayer and work.

But once we actually try to bring to God the needs of the Church and of the World, we confront head on, almost cruelly, our inability to do all that is so desperately required. Immediately we are face to face with our human frailty, impotence and helplessness. We know what they mean who say the intercessor stands in the gap between God and Man and can only cry 'Lord have mercy'.

Face these feelings of frustration and impotence frankly. Intercession is an overwhelming task which brings its own particular pain. We are bound to ask a searching question. What is the point of spending time in intercession if we can expect to achieve what, in human terms, is so little?

Facing these limitations as intercessors, however, is not as destructive as it sounds. It is a point to which God must bring us if we are to be released from being self-centred agents into self-giving agents of the Kingdom. This is the point where the temporary vision of God we are able to sustain regularly collapses and is remade. God must bring us to our own Gethsemane before we can go forward to do his work.

II

Another frustration we encounter in intercession is our inability to encompass within our prayers everything that needs our concern. But this too throws us away from self and back onto our reliance on God, in the best sense. Only he can order all things. We need to develop our understanding of God's providence; that constant loving care with which he sustains all things. What we are called on to do in intercession is to play a part and take a share within his work.

And those whom we, through ignorance or
forgetfulness or the number of names, have
not remembered, do Thou, O God,
remember them, who knowest the age and
the name of each one, who knowest each
from his mother's womb. For thou, O God,

> *art the help of the helpless, the hope of the*
> *hopeless, the saviour of the tempest-tossed,*
> *the harbour of mariners, the physician of the*
> *sick. Be thou thyself all things to all men,*
> *who knowest each and his petition and his*
> *dwelling and his need.*
>
> (The Liturgy of St Basil the Great)

Jesus offers us a picture of God for whom the fall of a sparrow does not go unnoticed, and this was the God to whom he prayed. When we intercede we are praying to a Faithful Creator, a Loving Father, and the One who rescues his people and saves mankind.

III

Jesus taught his disciples about the prayer of asking, in the night before he was betrayed, when they were filled with fear and apprehension. He said,

> *For the moment you are sad at heart; but I*
> *shall see you again, and then you will be*
> *joyful, and no one shall rob you of your joy.*
> *When that day comes you will ask nothing*
> *of me. In very truth I tell you, if you ask the*
> *Father for anything in my name, he will give*
> *it you. So far you have asked nothing in my*
> *name. Ask and you will receive, that your*
> *joy may be complete. (John 16).*

Three things from Jesus' teaching strengthen us. First, all intercessory prayer takes place 'When that day comes', which means the asking and the giving are part of the arrival (the coming) of the Kingdom.

Second, when that day comes we pray for ourselves with direct access to the Father, not through Jesus, and it is what we receive from the hand of the Father which is given to us 'in the name' of Jesus, and he enables us to receive it. Third, Jesus reveals the purpose of this kind of prayer. He says we should ask, confident we shall receive — 'that your joy may be complete'. Intercession is part of the Easter faith, its victory and rejoicing.

IV

How then does God ever 'answer' prayer, or are we using the wrong word for his response to our praying?

Jesus coupled his teaching about intercession with the words, 'Not as the world gives, give I unto you'. Thus our prayers of asking are held firmly within another aspect of the coming Kingdom; it is both 'Now and not yet'. Therefore the answers we receive contain the same eschatological tension as all the other signs of the Kingdom. What Jesus is anxious to teach us about intercession is that we should be brave enough constantly to ask, and trusting enough to believe that whatever God gives will indeed be what we require, rather than something inappropriate or harmful; even though for the present, every answer to intercession we receive can only be a foretaste, as it were, of what is still to come. However much our prayers are answered, there always remains within them, for the present, that which must remain 'unanswered'.

Thus the ultimate condition of intercessory prayer is knowing both our total dependence on

God and his total self-giving to us, at great cost to himself. Once we begin to glimpse that cost to God's Self, and the more we give ourselves in full contemplation of it and response to it, the more we shall know how our prayers are answered.

V

Intercession remains part of Christian prayer, all of which continues 'without ceasing'. Our requests to God are anchored in the continuing prayer of Christ and the Church. So the trigger for making intercession is not human need in the way we usually think of it, or the way the media brings it to our notice, but the great Act of Thanksgiving itself which is articulated in every eucharist. The whole eucharistic action is intercession — bringing the needs of God's world to him and bringing the healing touch of God to his world, within our thankful belief that the world is created, sustained and redeemed by God in his unending, forgiving love.

At every Eucharist the Prayer for the Church and for the World puts into words and concentrated form the desire for the coming of God's Kingdom among us, and our willingness to be used as agents of that Kingdom. It is this context of intercession which alone enables us always to pray with confidence.

Unless we get this clear, intercession can leave us with a sense of disappointment and frustration. But once we see it as an expression of trust and co-operation with God — the tip of the ice-berg of the continuous *work* of bringing in the kingdom *by God*

— then we can begin to see a role for ourselves to play, within the divine task. We are 'fellow-workers' with God. Through our prayer, he chooses to share the task with us, as he chose to share it with Jesus.

For further reading and thought

A Theme Word — Continuing

Michael Ramsey commended the Jesus-Prayer familiar to the Eastern Orthodox Church, with its ceaseless quiet repetition of 'Lord Jesus Christ, Son of the living God, have mercy upon me, a sinner'; and his inference from this takes us for a moment into the hidden place of his own practice of prayer.
The repetition, many times and many times, is found to quieten the distracting parts of our personalities and to keep us wonderfully subdued and concentrated, and as we repeat the words again and again we bring into our heart the many people and needs about whom we really want to pray. As the words proceed the heart has the people on it one by one.

(Owen Chadwick, *Michael Ramsey, a life.*)

Advice given to those who wonder how intercession can work or is it worthwhile:

1. Offer your own faith and love and readiness to hold to God come what may.

2. Offer your own faith that God is present and active in the world *and* in the life of those being prayed for.

3. Offer yourself as an instrument ready and willing to be used.

(Colin Semper)

If in the process of discovering where you stand in relation to God — how far you are an outsider — you come to the point of knocking, of going deeper and deeper into yourself, turning your prayer on yourself, bringing yourself to the point where there is a door to knock on, the point where it can be opened — there will come a moment when the door will open, but then you must have a name for God. You must be able to say a word that shows that it is you who have been in search of Him, and not an interchangeable human being in quest of an anonymous God.

(Anthony Bloom, *School for Prayer*)

The resurrection is for Christians the supreme sign that God does indeed act in this world to bring life out of death, hope out of despair, victory out of defeat, and vindication to those who trust in him. It is an invitation to live hopefully and to pray faithfully, because it shows us that just as we are free to 'do a new thing', so is God. Prayer is the exploration of that freedom, both God's and ours. It is the sending of our spirits beyond the realms of calculations, necessities and regularities, to the realm of openness with God and openness to God, where God's freedom to give or to withhold is openly and gladly acknowledged.

(John Habgood, *Letters on belief*)

God be praised, he gives us the victory through our Lord Jesus Christ. Therefore, my beloved brothers, stand firm and immovable, and work for the Lord always, work without limit, since you know that in the Lord your labour cannot be lost.

(1 Corinthians 15:57-58)

Music

Mozart, Symphony No 41, K 551 'The Jupiter' — among the best examples of musical inspiration at full tilt, where the beginning and end of the musical experience are joined by an inevitability and sense of completion and fulfilment.

Part Two

Called To Lead

A task suitable for beginners

Some are called not only to pray for others *with* the congregation but also to *lead* the congregation in prayer. Already we have noticed, how, within the Liturgy (the Eucharist), the highest value has always been placed on the Prayer of Intercession. Therefore, the person who has the task of leading the Prayers of the Faithful within the Ministry of the Word inevitably carries a great responsibility, every bit as weighty as reading scripture or preaching.

Conscious of this, the leader will draw heavily on his or her own experience of, and understanding of prayer. Therefore, like the preacher, he or she regularly confronts the poverty of Spirit within, even after considerable experience of undertaking the task.

This is bound to make it sound as though leading intercessory prayer is not something for beginners to tackle. Quite the opposite, in fact. Precisely because all Christians are beginners in some way or another and remain beginners throughout life, conversation with God, being with him, is all part of the unceasing life of discipleship and prayer into which we are called to grow with eagerness, courage and sensitivity. Those who are aware of being beginners in the exploration and adventure of praying, and are deliberately attempting to grow in prayer, will make good leaders. Those who have a misplaced confidence will be less useful.

This is not to say the leader should repeat the first thing that comes to mind, or be careless and thoughtless and speak off the top of the head. Never be afraid of thorough preparation. It's not only genius which is one per cent inspiration and ninety-nine per cent perspiration! Inspiration and spontaneity are not necessarily killed in the study. Winston Churchill used to memorise his impromptu speeches and even rehearse them in front of a mirror. Nevertheless the speeches remained, in a mysterious way, entirely spontaneous.

Nor need reluctance or inexperience be a barrier to an effective ministry of leadership. From Moses on, God has called and used many reluctant leaders. On the other hand, those who are eager to lead (too eager?) will need to be tested harder and further before they can be entrusted with the task.

The discipline of leadership

The exercise of any Christian ministry of leadership calls for particular qualities in a disciple. Because it is a vocation, the offering of leadership is first a response *to God* rather than to others. However desperate the need for leadership in the local church appears to be, until God calls any attempts we make to meet the need will get off to a bad start, if they start at all. The Church often has to *wait* in emptiness before God provides — sometimes for what seems a long time.

One reason why those taking up any ministry of leadership must always put vocation before need is that this is the only way to avoid what the hymn-writer means by his 'calling's snare'. We have to be honest and face the serious risk that any leader of intercession may try to hi-jack the service in a number of dangerous ways; all of which must be resisted.

For instance, there can be a strong temptation for the leader to turn the intercessions into a kind of mini-sermon (which I have known to last longer than the sermon itself). Or he or she may be tempted to try to correct the preacher, if there is disapproval of what has just been said. Or the leader may try to make up in some way for what the preacher didn't say and perhaps the leader feels ought to have been said.

There is also a genuine danger that the tone of voice the leader uses will attempt either to 'preach at', or instruct the congregation, or cajole them, instead of leading them all in their corporate prayer to God. I have even heard some who appear to be trying to bully God in the same way.

Worse, a leader may simply peddle private concerns and prejudices, sometimes coloured in a particular way politically, and obviously he or she will always have to guard against the lure of the sound of their own voice.

Finally, although, as we have said, the Church has always attached the greatest importance to the Prayers of the Faithful within the Liturgy, the intercession remains only an ingredient not the whole. If intercessory prayer is over emphasised, it destroys the balance of Word and Sacrament in the Eucharist — which is to hear scripture read and expounded, to pray for others as well as ourselves, and to share in the common meal. Each aspect of the Eucharist is inter-dependent and needs the other for its own sake. The task of the one who leads the intercession is to discipline himself or herself to make this time of special attentiveness alive as part of the full flow of the Liturgy.

One way to prevent the service getting out of balance through a wrong understanding of the intercession is to make sure there is plenty of scope privately and corporately for other forms of prayer at other times. Meditation and contemplation need not be sharply differentiated from intercession but nor should they be confused with it.

Training oneself to lead

Once a vocation from God is recognised and accepted within the Church, then it has to be defined and trained, which is bound to take time, effort and commitment.

Two things stand out. One is, those who offer leadership within the Christian community do so for the sake of others and therefore their role as leader is representative not individualistic. Anyone who leads intercession must remain alert to the danger of getting in the way instead of enabling others to worship and pray. The Taizé Community describes what it calls 'a generous common prayer' and asks, 'how can we pray together, yet leave each other free to be still and know God?' Any leader must accept this tension and work to hold the two together.

The second is, leaders must possess the capacity (which Jesus himself had in abundance) of pointing away from self to God. However charismatic the presence of Jesus was to those around him, whenever they reflected on the effect it had, they realised it drew them away from him but brought them close to God. Any leader needs the same gift, which enables God to draw the whole congregation (including the leader of the prayer) closer to himself.

Leaders, therefore, develop the capacity to listen before they speak, to balance words with silence, to couple acceptance with desire; so that, out of human longing and demanding expressed in prayer, there grows among the People of God the willingness gladly to receive what it is he gives.

Does he take sugar?

This particular BBC programme about those with handicaps reveals how easy it is to talk about someone as though they are absent rather than present. In the same way, one of the greatest errors made by leaders of intercession (ordained and lay) is to talk to the congregation about God, or to talk to the congregation about other people or even about themselves, instead of leading the whole congregation present in prayer with God. Whenever intercession is mis-directed, it turns into a kind of sacred gossip-column, sanctified and hallowed by the environment, and used to pass on information to the congregation which could and should be communicated in others ways.

It cannot be emphasised too often, *intercession should always be addressed to God not to the congregation.* Really rigorous discipline is needed in leading the Prayers of the Faithful not to treat God as the third party who may or may not be listening to what is going on in church. Do insist that others tell you fearlessly if you, as leader, break this rule.

For instance compare the following examples:

(A) Let us ask God to make us follow the commandment to love our neighbour and care for them, especially the members of the . . . club who are in church with us this morning and who are desperately in need of more helpers and new accommodation following the decision of the local council to take over the site for development.

(B) O God, kindle your spirit of love in us that we may serve one another with compassion and care, and quicken our consciences that we may give the help so much needed by the . . . club.

The first example (intended to be a caricature: but is it?) is clearly directed at the congregation rather than God and disguises recruitment, and probably political comment, as prayer, while the second is a prayer to the Father to stir up the gifts of the Spirit within his people.

There is one exception to the rule of addressing our words to God rather than the congregation. When intercession is introduced with a traditional phrase used as a bidding, it is addressed to the congregation. For example 'Let us pray for . . .'. But whenever such a bidding is used, it MUST be followed by silent prayer and not be mistaken for prayer itself. If you invite others to pray for something or someone, space must be given in which actually to pray so that they can do what the invitation asks.

The use of Biddings is the basis of the Prayer for the Church in rite A and rite B in the *Alternative Service Book*, but all too often they are mishandled and no time is given for prayer itself. The Bidding rambles on and becomes a kind of verbal substitute for praying, and too often the order of collect and people's response also gets muddled up. The correct order is: bidding (short and direct), space and time for prayer, the summarising collect, the versicle and response.

Group Preparation: Ready for Sunday

In the recent Doctrine Report, *We believe in God*, the authors say 'The total exposure of oneself in prayer can be almost a breaking apart of oneself: prayer for a suffering world may leave one appalled by that suffering'. Intercession can be a demoralising rather than a creative experience. So those who lead this prayer constantly need to remember they have to help people handle an aspect of prayer which can become an overwhelming and impossible task,which slips away from its proper status as part of the divine activity of bringing in the Kingdom.

One obvious and fundamental source of strength and purpose for leaders who wrestle with the task of intercession is to form a team which meets regularly for group preparation and for prayer. Any such group should include ordained and lay ministers. Ideally, it should meet each week, which means it needs to be given the highest priority and commitment by its members. If such a commitment once a week really is impossible, then a monthly meeting would be the minimum. What is of little use is a group meeting where attendance is unpredictable and haphazard.

The meetings will be primarily for prayer. But there will also be opportunity to do some other things. For instance, the group can collate and keep up-to-date what I have called in the next chapter 'the geography of local need'. Lists and information are vital for making intercession. Another task would be regularly to review what is happening during the intercession at the weekly Sunday Eucharist — is the pattern stale? is there need for new approaches such as those suggested below? is the Sunday intercession being supported adequately by prayer and action? is the intercession being under-played or over-played in the Liturgy? The group will also allow criticism of the leaders — speaking the truth in love. However hard it is for Christians to offer (and indeed receive) creative criticism, no effective leadership survives long without it.

Whatever happens on Sunday during the intercession needs support. It must be built into a larger framework if it is to develop and deepen. The group meeting will inevitably find itself in some sense or another 'overseeing' the intercessory prayer of the whole local Christian congregation.

For instance in every parish there will always be a number of people offering personal, private intercession who need to be encouraged. Some will be housebound and it is a great help for them to know they are praying with and alongside the more obvious and identifiable 'community'. One way of linking together all those who pray is to use a prayer booklet which gives a framework for a months intercession and supplement it with the weekly news-sheet which can contain immediate information.

The intercession at the weekly Eucharist will also be helped if it is built into (i) an annual cycle of prayer (such as the *Anglican Cycle of Prayer* published for the Anglican Consultative Council); (ii) a monthly cycle which will include more local concerns such as the institutions, hospitals and schools etc of the parish; and (iii) a weekly cycle which brings immediate needs to God in a regular sequence. Practical suggestions are offered in the next chapter, but it is the Parish Intercession Group which ought regularly to select and revise the material being used as the basis for the prayer of the Faithful.

Map-Work

A diary entry made by Winston Churchill shows how victory was planned in the Second World War.

On Monday 15th May 1944, three weeks before D-day, we held a final conference in London at Montgomery's headquarters in St Paul's School. The King, Fieldmarshall Smuts, the British Chiefs of Staff, the commanders of the expedition, and many of the principal staff officers were present. On the stage was a map of the Normandy beaches and the immediate hinterland, set at a slope so that the audience could see it clearly, and so constructed that the officers explaining the plan of operation could walk about on it and point out the landmarks.

When we hold up the action of the Eucharist by the long prayer for the whole Church and the world, we are in the map room, in conference about the strategy for the liberation of the souls of men and women. It needs only imagination and attention to bring the prayer to life. See the great map set before us: the map of the world with the Church in every place: every place and every person needing our help and our prayer.

As we have already said, to lead intercession effectively, the leader needs detailed lists and information, carefully prepared and kept up to date. The basic framework corresponds to the sections within the Prayer for the Church in the *Alternative Service Book*, rite A and rite B:

The Church
The World and its needs
The Family and neighbourhood
The Sick and suffering
The Departed

Other frameworks can be devised, for example:

based on the Lord's Prayer:

Vision (of heaven)
Kingdom (thy will be done on earth)
Providence (human need and daily bread)
Forgiveness (forgive us as we forgive)
Deliverance (liberation — freedom)

based on the Collect for Purity:

Openness — receiving — longing
Cleanse — forgiveness — healing — wholeness
Inspiration — vision — hope
Love and praise — adoration

based on the sections of Milner-White's *Daily Prayer*:

Daily Work
Peace
The Church
Unity
Suffering
Family

There will be other structures which you can adapt from bible-passages or from traditional prayers. But remember always that these particular frameworks are intended for intercession, not for meditation.

The Places on the Prayer-Map

1 The Church and the Christian family.
This will first have both a national and local dimension. Usually each diocese in the Anglican Communion produces its own annual Calendar of Intercession which links the local diocese with the national church. Many parishes also have a monthly intercession list, sometimes based on the areas and streets of the parish, and with parochial and local organisations and officers prayed for on a regular basis. There will also be an international dimension. The annual *Anglican Cycle of Prayer* mentioned earlier is useful, with subjects for intercession and also some detailed background information to fill them out with setting, context and meaning.

Care should be taken not to give the impression that prayer for the Anglican Community is the same as prayer for the world-wide Church. An ecumenical dimension to prayers for the Church will guard against this kind of parochialism.

It's worth taking care not to allow this section of the prayer to outweigh the others in length and detail, giving the impression that prayer for the Church is more important than prayer for the world and those in need, who can be dismissed almost as an afterthought in half the time.

2 The world and its needs.
The obvious danger here is to include too much,
or to be too vague. In keeping the lists of human
need up to date, remember to give the items
priorities within priorities and provide a basis for
rotation of subject and theme. Try not to pray for
the same sort of human concerns too often (i.e.
reconciliation and peace are not the only needs of
mankind).

Also, remember that the priorities of the media
headlines are not necessarily the priorities of
Christian prayer. The hard task is to keep concern
alive and active. Precisely because the needs of the
world are so widely known through the media, there
is a great tendency to 'switch off' when they are
mentioned ('yet again'?).

One useful tip to bring prayer for the world to
life is always to humanise geography. For example,
remember it was Moses who led the Israelites out
of Egypt. (Be careful though not to overload the
prayer with so much detail that you need a compass
to follow it).

3 The local community.
There may be a danger here that the names and
needs will overlap with section (1) for the Church.
Quite a lot of research will be needed, e.g. to find
out the names of local councillors, details of local
organisations, schools, hospitals etc., and keep them
up to date.

**4 A list of those in special need, sickness and
bereavement.**
Above all, in this section remember the need to

respect people's privacy. Some will not want personal details about themselves to be made public. A basic rule is to pray only for those who ask for prayer, or to check first that someone is happy for their name to be added to the intercession list.

In nearly every case, names should be used in intercession; but it is not always necessary to add surnames except when it helps to identify the person. To preserve anonimity, or to pray for someone whose name is unknown, the biblical names Mary and John are often used. Titles should never be used in intercession, although it is customary to add the word, bishop, priest or deacon where it applies.

Prayer for the sick should be particular in detail, wherever possible, but remember the details, of an operation for example, should be very brief, direct and specific(and has already been said, sensitive to privacy).

Among the names of the sick, it is necessary to make a distinction between those who are long-term patients and those who are not. The chronically sick will probably be prayed for over several years, of course, but perhaps only on, say, the first Sunday of the month rather than at every Eucharist. Another method some parishes use is to give a weekday eucharist a special intention of Prayer for the chronically sick. Each parish will need to decide its own way of handling the prayers for the sick.

The hungry, the homeless, the bereaved, those in prison, and others in special need should be included in this section. Again, a balance between the sick, and others in need, needs to be struck and held, otherwise it may appear that Christians are only concerned with illness.

5 The Christian family departed.
This list will include the names of those who have died recently, although it will be necessary to decide how long they should remain on it. Should it be for a week, a fortnight or a month?

Then the list will include those whose Year's Mind, (anniversary of the date of death), falls within the week. Each parish can assemble such a list, either from parish records and/or from the All Souls-tide list, and from requests from the congregation for names to be included. Care should be taken here about the names which are included. I hope it is unnecessary to spell it out, but pets and animals should not be included (although I have known some parisioners attempt to put them in).

The *Alternative Service Book* has a useful pair of phrases which encompasses all who have died — 'the faithful departed' and 'those whose faith is known to God alone' — and although it is never the task of the leader of intercession to make a judgment of any kind, it is worth remembering that sometimes one phrase will be more appropriate than the other.

This is also the section in which to com-memorate the names from the Church's calendar of saints, and it is well worth attempting to build up a list of local saints (in the New Testament sense of all Christian people) from the centuries of

Christian history, although it will require a good deal of skill to find the information. But such a list does give considerable depth to the commemoration, if it includes Christians from across several centuries and not only from the present and the distant past.

How is the prayer built up?

We have said it begins by gathering information. A notebook will obviously be essential, and a loose-leaf book the easiest kind to use. Set up the sections under the headings listed above.

Hopefully some basic map-work will have been provided either by the parish priest or a small group working on it in the first place. These topics will then be supplemented by gleaning further information from the TV and radio, from newspapers — local as well as national, from the parish magazine and the weekly news-sheet. Many parishes have an intercessions-board or box which should also be used as a resource. One difficulty is timing. Don't worry unduly if 'late items' come in after you have prepared your intercession. It's easy enough to add names at the last minute, but unnecessary to be so up-to-date that the material is rushed and badly prepared. Intercession is already being made to God on our behalf by the risen Christ: it's good to know it doesn't all depend on our ability to keep pace.

Gathering information, however is not enough. A knack of selection is vital. Some things will have to be left out from time to time, and a rota-basis provided for them so that they are not forgotten. The subjects for prayer you use need to be carefully balanced so that the sections don't become unwieldy. Sorting the information into the correct sections of the prayer also requires care. For instance, those who are bereaved should come in section 4 not section 5. Unless this is carefully thought through beforehand, the intercession can become confusing and muddled.

Another method is to make a scrap-book, and keep in it pictures, photos, cuttings, requests for prayer, and any other notes you think you can use to build the prayer.

Finding the words

The best advice here is to study examples. For instance there are new intercessions in *Patterns for Worship* (Section 4:5, pages 136 ff); in *Springboard to Worship* by Susan Sayers (which includes intercessions on the Sunday themes of the ASB, Years 1 and 2); in the Taizé book, *Praying Together in Word and Song* (there are several excellent examples of intercession here, but most of the book is about how to organise meetings for prayer rather than leading the Prayers of the Faithful at the Eucharist and this distinction should not be overlooked).

Use short words wherever possible, and indeed, use short sentences. Write out the words you want to use and then (as an exercise, if nothing else) precis them to half the length and see how much, if anything, you have left out and needs to be brought back into the prayer. Also, always remember the difference between written and spoken speech and discard words which are right in written prose but are rarely spoken in everyday language.

Do not begin prayer with 'Let us pray for ...' because immediately you are talking to the congregation and not God. Instead use the phrase, 'Father we pray to you...' or 'O God of love we bring to you ...' or 'we ask you' or better still, 'Bless O Lord ...' or 'Protect Father ...' The injunctions 'bless', 'guide', 'help' 'sustain' are short, crisp and clear; but they do open up one danger — make sure you avoid giving God instructions.

Finally, beware of using other peoples words, or phrases from familiar collects, or quotations. These tend to be artificial. God wants us to speak with him using our own words as much as we can.

—— Practical Hints and Tips ——

1. How to get started? Don't be afraid to use the set form to begin with which will help you get used to standing up there and hearing your own voice. There are several useful alternatives from which to choose set out in the next Chapter. Then when you move on, always write down the intercessions you propose to use in full, though on the day you will probably either depart from the prepared text or use a second version using only headings based on the original prayers.

2. Try to keep a balance between the general and the specific. But also try to make the intercessions an expression of the corporate life of the community, not just a list of individuals and their private concerns.

3. Although there is no need to start every petition with an act of thanksgiving, it is always good to hold human need within an awareness of divine providence. For example, when we pray for the sick it's worth giving thanks for the health which God has already provided, and which is perhaps being taken for granted and going un-noticed.

The collects in the Book of Common Prayer (most of which are based on ancient prayers) illustrate this basic structure for prayer in a concise way. For instance, read the collect for The Fourth Sunday of Easter in the Book of Common Prayer. It begins, 'O Almighty God, who alone canst order the unruly wills and affections of sinful men'. That is the basis of the prayer — God's sovereignty over his creation. Spend time quietly looking at other collects and write down a sentence which sums up on which characteristic of God the prayer rests. This 'home-work' or study will help us to discover how to link our praying with the nature of God.

4. A golden rule for leading prayer at the Eucharist — *do not be too long*, and remember the skill of artists and musicians who know what to leave out as well as what to put in. Accept the limits of the time available positively, and realise we are not meant to pray for everything all at once anyway. Deliberate concentration on some things, and the discipline of using a rota or sequence of prayer over several weeks, is part of the way we are meant to intercede. Be especially careful if there has been an unexpectedly long sermon, or perhaps an extra reading. To plough on with the prepared prayer against all the odds is usually a mistake. A lengthy sermon is often helped by a shorter intercession, while, if the preacher has been concise and to the point, it would be good to expand the intercession which follows it.

5. Link the prayer with the Sunday theme, especially, of course, the seasonal themes, and (if possible) link it with the theme of the sermon just preached. Don't hesitate to have a piece of paper and a pencil available with you for use during the sermon.

6. Look for variety in the use of the prayer — remember the framework is only there to help and it is permissable to omit some of the traditional sections of the prayer from time to time, (this may help timing), or to read the prayer straight through with no additional material.

7. Audibility and posture. Make sure you can be heard. There is nothing worse for a member of the congregation than to be invited to pray and then not be able to hear or follow the subjects for prayer. Work out carefully the best place from which to lead the prayer, bearing in mind the need for audibility — e.g. the lectern, a prayer-desk in the body of the church, or a stall in the choir etc. You will almost always be heard better if you stand while you are speaking. If you are expected to use micro-phones do spend time rehearsing and remember amplification only amplifies. Defects remain defects and are only made louder and more noticeable by the machine — they are not rectified mechanically. If you need help and advice, don't be shy or nervous about looking for it.

8. Different voices can be used in the prayer, of course — one for the bidding, another for the collect, another for the versicle and response. For instance,

Voice 1:   Let us pray for …
             (the bidding addressed to the congregation)

Voice 2:   Almighty God …
             (the collect addressed to God)

Voice 3:   Lord, we pray:
             (a versicle)

Congregation: Your kingdom come, your will be done.
             (a response)

Usually it is practical to limit the number of voices to no more than four, and when this happens, make sure *all* who are to speak can be heard. When the voices are scattered in various parts of the church, you won't be able to do without a rehearsal, even if all the participants are experienced, if you want to make sure this method works.

9. If the congregation is being asked to take part in a new form of intercession, make sure the people know what you are going to do before you start the prayer (especially if you are integrating music into the prayer in some way — see below).

Make any instructions you give neat and tidy. This is not the time to think on your feet. If you haven't got it clear in your mind what is to happen, you will almost certainly confuse others when you are explaining to them what to do.

It is usually best to describe what will happen BEFORE the people kneel or stand. It is also possible to 'rehearse' briefly, by inviting the congregation to repeat the response before the intercession begins. More than two responses cannot be memorised easily at one time. Only when all are informed and confident about what is to happen should you give whatever customary invitation to prayer you use or say 'Let us pray'. People must know what is going on if they are to share in it.

If the instructions are printed on the weekly news-sheet, again make sure they are clear and brief.

10. Use of silence. This is often overlooked and yet remains one of the basic ingredients in all intercession because it gives the time and space needed for prayer. As we have seen, originally in the Solemn Prayers on Good Friday, silence was kept after each bidding. If the Church is to rediscover the power of intercession, it is essential to regain the ability to pray without words, corporately as well as individually.

Again congregations will almost certainly need help and instruction — in sermons and preparation groups. The leader will need to develop the sensitivity to create times of silence which are not too short to be of use or too long to be embarrassing (especially if children are present), although noise (from children, for example) need not 'disturb' the silence. After all the purpose of keeping silence is not to shut out what is going on but actually to listen and hear — perhaps for the first time — what we usually ignore, which might indeed be the children of the Church.

To begin using silence in prayer, it is a useful tip to keep a time of silence at the end of the intercession. This can be introduced with a phrase such as — 'in silence we bring our own requests to God and pray for one another', or 'let us pray together in silence'. The leader needs also to be sensitive and vary the length of the silence kept. Sometimes a brief moment will be 'a huge silence', sometimes it will take longer to create it.

11. Spontaneous prayer and added petitions from the congregation. This is almost as difficult (to begin with) as introducing silence into prayer,

but once it has been developed it will become perfectly natural and easy. This too will obviously require instruction and training. Almost always it will be best to put it into practice first in a small group, perhaps in a house group, or a mid-week prayer group or at a weeknight Eucharist. People can be encouraged to grow in confidence in various ways. For instance, begin while sitting together in prayer rather than kneeling. Don't worry if, at first, eyes are open instead of shut (this helps to get used to noticing when to speak and when not to speak, so that the fear of interrupting another begins to evaporate). Develop the aural sensitivity to listen to others and the attitude of mind that a group of individuals are praying together.

The task of the leader on these occasions is to invite others to put their intercessions into words, to create a sense of security and calm, not to be worried by silence, and to draw the prayer to a suitable conclusion when the time comes. Probably this sort of prayer will not become a regular feature of the Prayers of the Faithful at the Sunday morning eucharist, but it would be a great enrichment to intercession if it could be used from time to time.

11. The use of music. There are two approaches to this. One is to use music as a background or back-cloth to some times of prayer. It can be instrumental or vocal music, live or pre-recorded. Music clearly creates an atmosphere of reflection and devotion: a useful base from which to begin to pray. Using pre-recorded music needs detailed preparation and good sound equipment. Remember we are all used to the experts handling complex audio systems on radio and TV and we find the second-rate irritating

and distracting — not a good frame of mind for praying. Nevertheless although we needn't expect to reproduce a BBC studio — and the simplest equipment can often be best — what matters is handling it successfully, which always requires careful preparation. Sadly this is why so often the maxim remains, if you can't do it well, don't do it at all. And yet, so much can be gained if the extra effort is made to 'do it well' and get it right in the first place.

The other way to use music in intercession is to sing a short musical refrain at the beginning and the end of the prayer, and to sing the response after each petition. Many will know the Taizé melody:
O Lord hear my prayer, O Lord hear my prayer:
when I call answer me.

This is effective, either as a response throughout the prayer, or as a repeated song with a crescendo and diminuendo before the intercession begins. Other examples of short pieces of music which are suitable before or after intercession, from the Taizé Community and elsewhere are printed in the last section of this book. There is a considerable variety of people's responses available for use in intercession. Care should be taken to select a piece suitable to the season of the Church's year or the overall purpose of the particular intercession e.g., is it penitence, thanksgiving, joy or sorrow?

When music is used like this, the phrase to be sung cannot be elaborate and the accompaniment must be simple, played perhaps on piano or guitar which can be less heavy than the organ (a solo flute or recorder can be helpful). Again take care that the accompaniment is not a distraction or irritation. Unaccompanied singing can be the most effective and musical.

12. The use of visual aids and lighting. This too can open up new ways into intercession. Now the TV and the press are dominated less and less by words and more and more by pictures, one of the difficulties about the traditional intercession in church is that it can be far too *wordy*. If you are going to use visual aids and lighting effects, again, make sure they work. Thorough preparation remains the key to success. If a screen is to be used, it might be possible to site it either at the back of the church or between one of the pillars rather than at the front, above or beside the altar, which is bound to be distracting for the rest of the service. Worse still would be to dismantle it during the service. The congregation can be asked to turn to face the screen for the Prayers, and there is no reason why people shouldn't stand to pray on this occasion. Two or three visual images will usually be sufficient to keep the interest and arouse the imagination and concern during such a time of prayer. Do avoid the danger of allowing the whole experience to become impossibly complicated and over ambitious.

Forms of Intercession

In the *Alternative Service Book* there are forms of intercession on pages 99 ff. The Litany (not all of it need be used at once and some sections are very helpful when used alone) pages 124' and 166-9 (rite A); and pp. 183-6 (rite B).

Here are two forms from other churches:

1. The Church of Ireland (1984)

Minister: Let us pray.

Almighty God, our heavenly Father,
you promised through your Son Jesus
    Christ
to hear the prayers of those who ask
    in faith:

We pray for your Church in all the
    world

for this diocese ... and for ... our
    bishop
for ...

Grant that we, and all who
    confess your name,
may be united in your truth,
live together in your love,
and reveal your glory in the
    world.

Lord, in your mercy
Hear our prayer.

78

We pray for the nations of the
world . . .
for this country . . . and for . . . our
Queen, (President)

for all in authority
and for the communities in which we
live and work . . .

> Guide the people of this land
>   and of all the nations,
> in the ways of justice and of
>   peace,
> that we may honour one another
> and serve the common good.
>
> Lord, in your mercy
> **Hear our prayer.**

We pray for the sick . . . the
poor . . .
and those in trouble . . . and for . . .

> Save and comfort all who suffer,
> that they may hold to you
>   through good and ill,
> and trust in your unfailing love.
>
> Lord, in your mercy
> **Hear our prayer.**

We bless your holy name for all your
servants
who have died in faith (for . . .)

The Pleasure of God's Company

We rejoice in the faithful witness
    of your people
in every age, and pray that we
    may share with them
the joys of your eternal kingdom.

Merciful Father,
**Accept these our prayers
for the sake of your Son
our Saviour Jesus Christ.   Amen**

**2. The Lima Liturgy (1982) World Council of
Churches**
Minister: In faith let us pray to God our
            Father,
           his Son Jesus Christ
           and the Holy Spirit.

Kyrie Eleison

For the Church of God throughout
    the world,
let us invoke the Spirit.

Kyrie Eleison

For the leaders of the nations,
that they may establish and defend
    justice and peace,
let us pray for the wisdom of God.

Kyrie Eleison

Examples and resources

For those who suffer oppression or
    violence
let us invoke the power of the
    Deliverer.

Kyrie Eleison

That the churches may discover again
    their visible unity
in the one baptism which
    incorporates them in Christ,
let us pray for the love of Christ.

Kyrie Eleison

That the churches may attain
    communion
in the eucharist around one table,
let us pray in the strength of Christ.

Kyrie Eleison

That the churches may recognise
    each other's ministries
in the service of their one Lord,
let us pray for the peace of Christ.

Kyrie Eleison

Into your hands, O Lord,
we commend all for whom we pray,
trusting in your mercy;
through your Son, Jesus Christ our
    Lord.   **Amen.**

Litanies

1. The Church of Ireland (1984)

Minister: Let us pray.

Almighty and everliving God
hear the prayers which we offer in
 faith:

For peace, and for the salvation of
 all men,
Lord, in your mercy
Hear our prayer.

For the one holy catholic and
 apostolic Church,
and for the unity of all Christian
 people,
Lord, in your mercy
Hear our prayer.

For all who minister in the church,
for bishops, priests and deacons,
Lord, in your mercy
Hear our prayer.

For those who learn and those who
 teach the Christian faith,
Lord, in your mercy
Hear our prayer.

For all who live and work in this
 parish,
Lord, in your mercy
Hear our prayer.

For families, and for those who live
  alone,
Lord, in your mercy
Hear our prayer.

For the sick and afflicted, and for
  those who care for them,
Lord, in your mercy
Hear our prayer.

For all in authority, and especially
  for ...
Lord, in your mercy
Hear our prayer.

For those who work for peace, justice
  and rightiousness
throughout the world,
Lord, in your mercy
Hear our prayer.

For ...
Lord, in your mercy
Hear our prayer.

Rejoicing in the fellowship of your
holy apostles and martyrs, and of all
your servants departed this life in
your faith and fear, we commend
ourselves and one another and our
whole life to you, Lord God; through
Jesus Christ our Saviour.   **Amen.**

2. A form for use with Rite A

President: In peace let us pray to the Lord;

All: **Lord, have mercy.**

President: For peace from on high and for the salvation of our souls, let us pray to the Lord;

All: **Lord, have mercy.**

President: For the holy Church of God in this land and throughout the world, that it may be filled with truth and love, let us pray to the Lord;

All: **Lord, have mercy.**

President: For ... our Bishop, for ... that they may continue to receive God's blessings in abundance, let us pray to the Lord;

All: **Lord, have mercy.**

President: For this holy place and house of prayer, for ... and for all who with faith, reverence and godly fear enter and worship here, let us pray to the Lord;

All: **Lord, have mercy.**

President: For the peace of the world, for those in authority in all the nations, especially for Elizabeth our Queen, let us pray to the Lord;

All: **Lord, have mercy.**

President: For the sick, the suffering, the sorrowful and the dying, let us pray to the Lord;

All: **Lord, have mercy.**

Examples and resources

President: For the poor, the hungry, the lonely
and the unemployed; for refugees,
prisoners and those who suffer
persecution, let us pray to the Lord;
All: **Lord, have mercy.**

President: Hear us O Lord as we remember
those who have died in the peace of
Christ, both those who have
confessed the faith and those whose
faith is known to you alone, and
grant us a share in your eternal
kingdom;
All: **Lord, have mercy.**

President: Rejoicing in the fellowship of the
Blessed Virgin Mary and all your
saints, we commend ourselves and all
Christian people to your unfailing
love.

Merciful Father,
All: **Accept these prayers
for the sake of your Son,
our Saviour Jesus Christ.** **Amen.**

3. The Book of Common Worship (Church of South India) (1962)
Minister: For the peace that is from above, and
for the salvation of your souls, let us
pray to the Lord
Lord, have mercy.

For the peace of the whole world, for
the welfare of God's holy churches,
and for the union of all, let us pray
to the Lord
Lord, have mercy.

For our bishops, and all other
ministers, especially ... our
Moderator, and ... our Bishop, that
with a good heart and a pure
conscience they may accomplish
their ministry, let us pray to the Lord
Lord, have mercy.

For the rulers of our country and all
in authority, let us pray to the Lord
Lord, have mercy.

For the sick, the suffering, the
sorrowful, and the dying, let us pray
to the Lord
Lord, have mercy.

For the poor, the hungry, orphans and
widows, and them that suffer
persecution, let us pray to the Lord
Lord, have mercy.

For ourselves and all who confess the
name of Christ, that we may show
forth the excellence of him who
called us out of darkness into his
marvellous light, let us pray to the
Lord
Lord, have mercy.

That, with all his servants who have served him here and are now at rest, we may enter into the fullness of his unending joy, let us pray to the Lord. **Lord, have mercy.**

Almighty God, the Fountain of all wisdom who knowest our necessities before we ask, and our ignorance in asking: We beseech thee to have compassion upon our infirmities; and those things, which for our unworthiness we dare not, and for our blindness, we cannot ask, vouchsafe to give us, for the worthiness of thy Son, Jesus Christ our Lord.

or   Almighty and everlasting God, by whose Spirit the whole body of the Church is governed and sanctified: Receive our supplications and prayers, which we offer before thee for all estates of men in thy holy Church, that every member of the same in his vocation and ministry, may truly and godly serve thee; through our Lord and Saviour, Jesus Christ.   **Amen.**

or   The grace of the Lord Jesus Christ, and the love of God and the fellowship of the Holy Spirit, be with us all.   **Amen.**

A Selection of Alternative Responses

In faith we pray to you our God
We pray to you our God

Lord, have mercy
Lord, have mercy

Lord in your mercy
hear our prayer.

Hear us
hear us, good Lord

Lord hear us
Lord graciously hear us

For ... let us pray to the Father
in Christ our Lord

Jesus, Lord of ... (a phrase which can be varied)
in your mercy, hear us.

(from *Patterns for Worship*)

—— Further Resources ——

1. These publications contain examples of intercessions and are useful to help the leader prepare further intercessions:

    Colin Semper, *Intercessions for use with Series 1 & 2 or Series 3 Holy Communion Services,* (Mowbray 1981)
    Raymond Hockley, *Intercessions at Holy Communion on themes for the Church's Year,* (Mowbray 1981)

2. These publications are also useful
    Susan Sayers, *Springboard to Worship,* (Kevin Mayhew 1989)
    Wild Goose Worship Group, *A wee Worship Book,* (Iona Community 1989)
    Praying Together in word and song, (second revised edition, Mowbray 1987)

Musical Settings of
Responses to Intercession

KYRIE ELEISON

**From an ancient
Russian Orthodox source**

(8) Ky - ri - e e lei - son, Ky - ri - e e -

(8)

lei - son, Ky - ri - e e - le - - - i - son.

KYRIE ELEISON   **JAQUES BERTHIER**

Optional descant

Ky - ri - e, Ky - ri - e e - le - i - son.

Ky - ri - e, Ky - ri - e e - le - i - son____

LORD OF THE CHURCH

PAUL ILES

IN OUR DARKNESS   JAQUES BERTHIER

© Les Presses de Taizé (France)
Published by Wm Collins and Sons Ltd

MY SOUL IS AT REST   JAQUES BERTHIER

STAY WITH US, O LORD JAQUES BERTHIER

O LORD, HEAR MY PRAYER   JAQUES BERTHIER

Published by Wm Collins and Sons Ltd

GOD OUR SAVIOUR   WILLIAM WHITEHEAD

God our Sa-viour,

— you know us and love us, and hear our prayer: — keep us in the e-ter-nal

fell-ow-ship — of Je - sus Christ ——— our Sa - viour. A - men.

Book List and Further Reading

1. Church of England Liturgical Commission, *The Presentation of the Eucharist,* (SPCK 1971) p. 12
2. Michael Perham, *The Eucharist,* (Alcuin Club Manual No 1., SPCK 1978) p. 7 ff & App. 2 p. 52 ff.
3. E.C. Whitaker, *The Intercessions of the Prayer Book,* (SPCK 1956) p. 36 ff. Appendix p. 62 ff.
4. J. Neville Ward, *The Use of Praying,* (Epworth Press 1967) Chapter 9 *Desiring Other People's Good*
5. Peter Baelz, *Does God answer prayer?* (Darton, Longman and Todd 1982)
6. Peter Baelz, *Prayer and Providence,* (SCM Press 1968)
7. Charles Elliott, *Praying the Kingdom,* Chapter — Prayer & the Worshipping Community
8. ed. Kenneth Stevenson, *Liturgy Reshaped,* Chapter 3, Intercession at the Eucharist (SPCK 1981)
9. The Joint Liturgical Group, *Getting the Liturgy Right,* (SPCK 1982)
10. Eric Milner-White, *Daily Prayer,* (OUP 1941) Appendix on *The form and structure of prayers.*